Good Habits

HBR EMOTIONAL INTELLIGENCE SERIES

HBR Emotional Intelligence Series

How to be human at work

The HBR Emotional Intelligence Series features smart, essential reading on the human side of professional life from the pages of *Harvard Business Review*.

Authentic Leadership	*Influence and Persuasion*
Confidence	*Leadership Presence*
Dealing with Difficult People	*Mindful Listening*
Empathy	*Mindfulness*
Energy and Motivation	*Power and Impact*
Focus	*Purpose, Meaning, and Passion*
Good Habits	*Resilience*
Happiness	*Self-Awareness*
Inclusion	*Virtual EI*

Other books on emotional intelligence from *Harvard Business Review*:

HBR Everyday Emotional Intelligence

HBR Guide to Emotional Intelligence

HBR's 10 Must Reads on Emotional Intelligence

Good Habits

HBR EMOTIONAL INTELLIGENCE SERIES

Harvard Business Review Press

Boston, Massachusetts

Copyright 2023
Harvard Business School Publishing Corporation
All rights reserved

Printed in the United States of America

10 9 8 7 6 5 4 3 2 1

No part of this publication may be reproduced, stored in or introduced into a retrieval system, or transmitted, in any form, or by any means (electronic, mechanical, photocopying, recording, or otherwise), without the prior permission of the publisher. Requests for permission should be directed to permissions@harvardbusiness.org, or mailed to Permissions, Harvard Business School Publishing, 60 Harvard Way, Boston, Massachusetts 02163.

The web addresses referenced in this book were live and correct at the time of the book's publication but may be subject to change.

Library of Congress Cataloging-in-Publication data is forthcoming.

ISBN: 978-1-64782-503-4
eISBN: 978-1-64782-504-1

The paper used in this publication meets the requirements of the American National Standard for Permanence of Paper for Publications and Documents in Libraries and Archives Z39.48-1992.

Contents

Contents

Contents

Good Habits

HBR EMOTIONAL INTELLIGENCE SERIES

1

What Does It Really Take to Build a New Habit?

By Kristi DePaul

Our habits govern our lives, literally. Research shows that around half of our daily actions are driven by repetition.[1] This is probably why behavioral scientists and psychologists have spent so much time writing about how to establish and keep positive habits. Regular sleep and exercise, a healthy diet, an organized schedule, and mindfulness are just a few examples of practices that—if done regularly—can improve our work, relationships, and mental health.

But what if those things don't come naturally to you? What does it take to build a new habit?

While there are plenty of hacks on the internet competing to answer these questions, the neuroscience behind habit formation doesn't offer shortcuts. Experts advocate for the old-fashioned approach: incremental progress. Dedicated commitment is what, time and again, has proven to lead to change.

Surprisingly, the first step toward creating long-term change involves building routines—not habits themselves.

Routines versus habits

Most of us assume the two are interchangeable. But Nir Eyal, author of *Indistractable: How to Control Your Attention and Choose Your Life*, told me that this is a common fallacy—one that tends to end in disappointment. "When we fail at forming new patterns of behavior, we often blame ourselves," he said, "rather than the bad advice we read from someone who doesn't really understand what can and cannot be a habit."

Eyal explained that a habit is a behavior done with little or no thought, while a routine involves a series of behaviors frequently, and intentionally, repeated. A behavior has to be a regularly performed routine before it can become a habit at all.

The problem is that many of us try to skip the "routine" phase. According to Eyal, this is because we think that habits will allow us to put tedious or unenjoyable tasks on autopilot. (Your to-do list would be so much better if it just conquered itself somehow.)

It makes sense.

Unlike habits, routines are uncomfortable and require a concerted effort. Waking up early to run every morning or meditating for 10 minutes every night, for instance, are rituals that—initially—are hard to keep up. Habits, on the other hand, are so ingrained in our daily lives that it feels strange not to do them. Imagine not brushing your teeth before bed or not drinking a cup of coffee with breakfast. If these are habits you have already formed, avoiding them might even feel bad.

To attempt to turn a routine into a habit, take the following steps.

Set your intentions

Keep in mind that some routines may blossom into habits, but not all of them can or will. Some things, while quantifiable, require too much concentration, deliberation, and effort to make the transition. For that reason, playing an instrument, cleaning your apartment, or journaling don't fall into the habit category; they're not effortless behaviors that can be done without conscious thought.

The point is: Pick the behavior you want to turn into a habit wisely. Maybe you want to drink more water throughout the day or skip checking your email first thing in the morning. Whatever you choose, be realistic about the process. It will take patience, self-discipline, and commitment.

"There's no such thing as 21 days to start a new habit," Charles Duhigg, author of *The Power of Habit*, told me. "The amount of time it takes will vary from person to person." Developing a pleasurable habit, like eating chocolate for breakfast, for instance, may take a day, while trying to exercise at 5 p.m. each evening may take much longer.

Ximena Vengoechea, a UX researcher and author of the book *Listen Like You Mean It*, added, "Reflect on what you're trying to achieve and why. Say your goal is to be a writer. Are you interested in writing a novel for fame, prestige, or money? Is it to gain the acceptance or love of someone you care about? Or is it simply because you love the craft?"

Understanding the "why" will help you stay motivated when inevitable roadblocks to building new routines surface.

Prepare for roadblocks

Reflect on why, to date, you haven't regularly practiced this behavior. What has stopped you in the past? Is fear or shame getting in the way? Or a lack of time?

"Familiarize yourself with your own blockers now so that you can quickly identify and manage them when they arise later on, because they will," Vengoechea said.

Maybe a busy schedule has kept you from hitting the gym every day. To avoid this occurrence from happening in the future, block 30 to 60 uninterrupted minutes on your calendar right now. Maybe you're just not feeling motivated enough lately. To keep yourself accountable, find an ally (or two) to share your goals with. This could be a trusted manager, peer, friend, partner, or family member.

"Make sure you share your ambitions, intentions, plans (and maybe even fears!) with someone who can support you and remind you of why you're taking this on in the first place when the going gets tough," Vengoechea said. Research shows that your odds of success increase dramatically when you make your intentions known to someone perceived to have a higher status than yourself or someone whose opinion you value.[2]

Start with nudges

You can put in place practical steps or nudges to help you kick off your new routine. Use one or all of the suggestions below to get organized and begin.

Make a schedule. Block regular times on your calendar (every day or every other day) to practice the behavior you want to build into a habit. Be sure not to overdo it initially. "If you dive in too fast and expect results right away," Vengoechea said, "odds are, you will fail and become discouraged before you even begin."

Set microhabits. In the spirit of keeping things simple, another option is to try out microhabits: incremental adjustments that (over time) move you closer to achieving your goals. Think of them like stepping stones that lead to your final destination. Here are a few examples to give you the idea:

The goal: Read more industry-related news.

What you can do: Create Google Alerts for topics directly related or even adjacent to your career interests, prompting you to click through and read at least one or two alerts every day.

The goal: Get better-quality sleep.

What you can do: Blue light from our screens hampers a good night's sleep. Keep your favorite books beside your bed, and leave your phone to charge in another room. When winding down for the night, you'll probably choose the nearby book instead of doom-scrolling.

The goal: Strengthen your network.

What you can do: Encourage yourself to reach out to others with visual cues. Put sticky notes with messages like "Did you show gratitude to a colleague today?" or "Reach out to someone new" on your screen as a way to remind yourself of your goal.

Try temptation bundling. This last type of nudge aims to make obligatory tasks more enjoyable. The concept itself was coined by researcher Katie Milkman and her colleagues, and it's fairly straightforward: Take an activity you don't like to do and something you do enjoy—then, bundle them together.

In practice, here's what temptation bundling can look like: Package a behavior that gives you instant gratification (checking TikTok, listening to music, or bingeing your favorite podcast series) with a beneficial, but less fun, activity (running on the treadmill, filling out a spreadsheet, or doing chores around the house). Only allow yourself to do the "fun" thing in tandem with the "not so fun" thing.

In Milkman's study, for example, the researchers gave participants iPods with four audio novels they wanted to listen to but could only access while working out. By and large, participants' gym attendance increased because it was tied to an indulgence.[3]

Show yourself compassion

Lastly, don't forget to be compassionate with yourself as you embark on this journey toward more thoughtful routines, and hopefully better habits. Any long-term change is going to take time. That's just the reality. There will be ups and downs. But you are capable, and if you've made it this far, you are also prepared.

Let the tools you've learned today be your compass. Let them guide you when you feel offtrack (which, by the way, is a totally normal feeling when you're trying something new).

Now, go get started.

KRISTI DEPAUL is a recognized expert on career navigation and personal branding whose writing has appeared in international outlets and has been cited by prominent think tanks and universities. She is the founder and principal at Nuanced, a thought leadership firm for executives, and serves as the CEO of Founders, a fully remote content agency focused on the future of learning and the future of work. She earned a master's degree from the H. John Heinz III College of Information Systems and Public Policy at Carnegie Mellon University.

Notes

1. David T. Neal, Wendy Wood, and Jeffrey M. Quinn, "Habits—A Repeat Performance," *Current Directions in Psychological Science* 15, no. 4 (2006): 198–202.
2. Howard J. Klein et al., "When Goals Are Known: The Effects of Audience Relative Status on Goal Commitment and Performance," *Journal of Applied Psychology* 105, no. 4 (2020): 372–389.

3. Katherine L. Milkman, Julia A. Minson, and Kevin G. M. Volpp, "Holding the Hunger Games Hostage at the Gym: An Evaluation of Temptation Bundling," *Management Science* 60, no. 2 (2013): 283–299.

Adapted from content posted on Ascend, hbr.org, February 2, 2021.

2

How to Break Up with Your Bad Habits

By Jud Brewer

B reaking habits is hard. We all know this, whether we've failed our latest diet (again) or felt the pull to refresh our Instagram feed instead of making progress on a work project that is past due. This is largely because we are constantly barraged by stimuli engineered to make us crave and consume, stimuli that hijack the reward-based learning system in our brains designed initially for survival.

Put simply, reward-based learning involves a trigger (for example, the feeling of hunger), followed by a behavior (eating food) and a reward (feeling sated). We want to do more of the things that feel good and less of the things that feel bad—or stressful. These three components (trigger, behavior, and reward) show up every time we smoke a cigarette or eat a cupcake. This is especially true at work. Each time we try to soothe ourselves from a taxing assignment we reinforce the reward, to the point where unhealthy distractions can become habits.

So why can't we just control ourselves and decide to replace bad habits with good ones? The doctrine of self-control has been promulgated for decades, despite the fact that researchers at Yale and elsewhere have shown that the brain networks associated with self-control (for example, the prefrontal cortex) are the first to go "offline" when faced with triggers such as stress.[1] Still, in medical school, I was taught to pass self-control rhetoric on to my patients. "Need to lose weight? Quit eating junk food. Trying to quit smoking? Stop cold turkey or use a nicotine replacement."

When I started actually practicing medicine, however, I quickly learned that it doesn't work this way in real life.

Self-control theories have missed something critical: Reward-based learning is based on rewards, not behaviors. How *rewarding* a behavior is drives how likely we are to repeat that behavior in the future. This is why self-control as an approach to breaking habits often fails.

Over the past 20 years, I've researched ways to create a better method by bringing the scientific and clinical practices together. My time spent studying the behavioral neuroscience of how habits form, and the best way to tackle them, helped me find a surprisingly natural way to do this: mindfulness.

By using mindfulness training to make people more aware of the "reward" reinforcing their behavior, I can help them tap into what is driving their habit in the first place. Once this happens, they are more easily able to change their association with the "reward" from a positive one to a more accurate (and often negative) one.

When someone joins our program to quit smoking, for example, the first thing I have them do is pay attention while they're smoking. They often give me a quizzical look, because they're expecting me to tell them to do something other than smoke, like eat candy as a substitute when they have a craving. But because a "reward" drives future behavior, and not the behavior itself, I have my clients pay attention to what it tastes and feels like when they smoke. The goal is to make the patient aware of the "reward value," or the level of positive reaffirmation, they are getting from the habit they want to change. The higher the value, the more likely they are to repeat the behavior.

I see the same thing happen over and over again—the reward value of the habit decreases because it isn't as gratifying as people remember. One client of mine, for instance, thought the act of smoking made her look cool as a teenager. Even though that motivation had dissipated in her adulthood, her brain still associated positive feelings with smoking. Hence, her reward value was high. When that same client started paying attention as she smoked, she realized that cigarettes taste bad, commenting, "Smells like stinky cheese and tastes like chemicals. Yuck." This helped her brain update the reward value of her habit. She was able to get accurate information about how smoking feels *right now*, which then helped her become disenchanted with the process.

After seeing how effective this practice was with my clients, I decided to test it even further. My lab and I developed three apps that deliver this same kind of mindfulness training to anyone with a smartphone via short sequential lessons over a period of three to four weeks. The apps are designed to help people break bad habits such as smoking, overeating, and anxiety (which, oddly enough, is driven by the same habit loops as the other two behaviors).[2]

Tens of thousands of people from around the world have used these apps, and my lab has published a number of studies showing significant, clinically meaningful results: five times the smoking quit rates of gold standard treatment, 40% reductions in craving-related eating, and a 63% reduction in anxiety.[3] In a recent randomized controlled trial, we even found that our mindfulness app for smoking cessation taught users how to better control the part of their brain that gets overactivated by smoking cues and chocolate cravings.[4]

While our research has been focused primarily on changing health-related habits, we believe it is highly relevant to the workplace. Our strategy can help workers up their productivity, morale, and overall performance by teaching them how to overcome the habits that may be holding them back from thriving. Here's how to get started.

1. Map out your habit loops

As I advise people in my outpatient clinic, the first step to breaking a habit (no matter what it is) is to figure out your triggers. If the habit is procrastination or stress eating at work, for example, pay attention to the circumstances surrounding you when you do those things. Do you have a big project you're trying to avoid? Do you have too much on your plate to manage?

Once you know your triggers, try to identify the behaviors you engage in when you are acting out. Do you check social media instead of doing work? Do you snack on sweets during challenging assignments? You must be able to name the actions you turn to for comfort or peace of mind before you can evaluate their reward values.

2. See what you actually get out of those actions

The next step is to clearly link action and outcome. Remember my patient who struggled to quit smoking? Just like I asked her to pay attention to the act of smoking, I am asking you to pay attention to how you feel when you partake in your habit.

If you stress eat, how does it feel to eat junk food when you aren't hungry? How does what you eat impact the state of your mind and body 15 minutes after the fact? If you procrastinate, what do you get from surfing the internet for pictures of cute puppies? How rewarding is it in the moment, especially when you realize that it isn't helping you get your work done?

Remember your answers to these questions, or write them down to help solidify them in your mind.

This new awareness you have developed will help your brain accurately update the reward value of the habit you want to break. You will begin to see that X behavior leads to Y consequences, and often those consequences are holding you back from reaching your full potential.

3. Replace the reward with curiosity

The final step to creating sustainable, positive habit change is to find a new reward that is more rewarding than the existing behavior. The brain is always looking for that bigger, better offer.

Imagine you are trying to break a bad habit like stress eating at work, and willpower hasn't quite worked out for you. What if, instead of indulging in your candy craving to counteract a negative emotion, you substituted it with curiosity about why you are having that craving in the first place and what it feels like in your body and your mind?

The reward value of curiosity (opening yourself up) is tangibly different than that of stress eating (closing yourself down) in this instance. Ultimately, curiosity feels better in the moment and is much more enjoyable than the rumination that often occurs after giving in to a bad habit.

To tap into their curiosity, I teach my patients a simple mantra: *Hmm.* As in, be curious about your feelings. What does this craving feel like when it first arrives, before I have decided to indulge it?

People often learn, pretty quickly, that cravings are made up of physical sensations and thoughts and that these come and go. Being curious helps them acknowledge those sensations without acting on them. In other words, they can ride the wave of a craving out by naming and sitting with the thoughts and feelings that arise in their bodies and minds from moment to moment—until those moments pass.

If you're curious to see how well this might work for you, now is a good time to give it a try.

The next time you find yourself indulging in a bad habit, take a moment to pause and consider using mindfulness to help you overcome it. Your behaviors may not change immediately—but stick with it. If you can hack your mind using our methods, you will eventually be able to break free of unwanted habits and comfortably watch your cravings pass by.

JUD BREWER is an addiction psychiatrist and neuroscientist specializing in anxiety and habit change. He is an associate professor at Brown University's School of Public Health and Medical School, chief medical officer at Sharecare, and the *New York Times* bestselling author of *Unwinding Anxiety* and *The Craving Mind.*

Notes

1. Amy F. T. Arnsten, "Stress Signalling Pathways That Impair Prefrontal Cortex Structure and Function," *Nature Reviews Neuroscience* 10 (2009): 410–422.
2. "The Anxiety Habit Loop," *Dr. Jud* (blog), March 15, 2020, https://drjud.com/how-anxiety-becomes-a-habit/.
3. Judson A. Brewer et al., "Mindfulness Training for Smoking Cessation: Results from a Randomized Controlled Trial," *Drug and Alcohol Dependence* 119, no. 1–2 (2001): 72–80; and Ashley E. Mason et al., "Testing a Mobile Mindful Eating Intervention Targeting Craving-Related Eating: Feasibility and Proof of Concept," *Journal of Behavioral Medicine* 41 (2018): 160–173.
4. Amy C. Janes et al., "Quitting Starts in the Brain: A Randomized Controlled Trial of App-Based Mindfulness Shows Decreases in Neural Responses to Smoking Cues That Predict Reductions in Smoking," *Neuropsychopharmacology* 44 (2019): 1631–1638; Amy C. Janes et al., "Insula–Dorsal Anterior Cingulate Cortex Coupling Is Associated with Enhanced Brain Reactivity to Smoking Cues," *Neuropsychopharmacology* 40 (2015): 1561–1568;

and Dana M. Small et al., "Changes in Brain Activity Related to Eating Chocolate: From Pleasure to Aversion," *Brain* 124, no. 9 (2001): 1720–1733.

Adapted from content posted on hbr.org, December 5, 2019 (product #H05B0D).

3

When Life Gets Busy, Focus on a Few Key Habits

By Jackie Coleman and John Coleman

Eight months ago, we welcomed our third child. Given that we've written about how to navigate careers, stress, and even annual planning as a couple, you'd think we'd be prepared for wonderful but disruptive life events like these. But as Mike Tyson famously quipped, "Everyone has a plan until they get punched in the mouth."

The past year has been a time of radical prioritization for us. We're constantly optimizing—identifying our most essential priorities and activities while reluctantly and painfully cutting things that are important but not urgent.

Maybe you're facing a life event that forces this type of radical prioritization. Whether it's changing jobs, taking care of a sick parent, relocating, or facing a difficult diagnosis, disruptions in life can make it hard to maintain moment-by-moment focus and well-being, much less think months or years into the future. Long-term goals remain important. But in the fog of life's most intense moments, long-term focus can be hard.

Daily or weekly habits aligned with your long-term goals can keep you on track even when it's hard to think ahead, and they can add stability in an otherwise unsteady time. Each of us have regular practices we try to maintain to give our lives structure, to remain mentally and physically healthy, and to assure we're approaching life consciously. These habits, important at any time, are essential in our busiest and most chaotic periods. So what do these habits look like?

The first step in maintaining regular habits is to articulate and track them. We find the key is to keep this simple. What are the five to 10 things you need to do daily or weekly to keep life on track? Once you've written them down, track them. The Momentum app, for example, is an easy way to set daily and weekly habits and be reminded of them. There are many others. You can also use a simple Excel spreadsheet or paper planner. The important thing is to reflect on the right habits, write them down, and stay accountable.

When setting habits, we've found the most critical are clustered in four key areas.

The first is *personal reflection*. This can look radically different depending on the person. For us, as people of faith, this involves prayer and scriptural study. It also includes religiously agnostic habits, like keeping diaries, documenting the funny things our children say, and crafting gratitude journals in which we can record what's happening in our lives and what we are grateful for multiple times per week. Studies have shown that these kind of practices can help us better process life events and remain joyful about the good we experience.

Relatedly, we need time for *professional reflection*. For years, John has maintained the same professional routine. He sits down on Sunday night with a weekly Moleskine planner and maps out his most important meetings and priorities for the week. This helps him assure he's focused on not simply what's most visible or immediate, but what's actually important. And it offers structure so that when new demands arise, he can more easily prioritize them. Then, each morning, he inserts a note card into the planner where he prioritizes what needs to be done that day. Simple, daily reflection on priorities and to-dos can make a meaningful difference in productivity and focus.

A third category of activities is *building and maintaining relationships*. Social science is crystal clear on the centrality of relationships to personal well-being. It's important to prioritize and manage relationships. For us, right now, the primary relationships we're focused on are with our kids and with each other. Each day, we structure a bedtime ritual with the kids where we all spend time together, reading and talking about our highs and lows. As a couple, we try to make time to speak every day and to get out of the house together, without the kids, once per week. We also each try to make at least some time to spend with a friend or two once a week. These sound like small things, but they can be critical to maintaining positive relationships and emotional well-being.

Finally, we all need to maintain habits that encourage *physical and mental health*. Studies show that people who get at least two days of exercise per week are happier (with each additional day boosting happiness further), as little as 20 minutes of exercise can boost mood, and 11 minutes of lifting weights can boost metabolic rate.[1] For mental health, daily meditation can be a lifesaver for restoring some order and balance in disordered and imbalanced times. Apps like Headspace and Calm have made practices like this more accessible than ever and easier to track and maintain. For both of us, the simple act of reserving 30 minutes each day for reading or writing can also promote mental health, a task that seems to be backed by science.[2]

Everyone's life looks different. But we all have periods of life that are busy, disordered, and stressful. In those times, short-term habits—weekly or daily practices—can trump long-term goals as a way to focus, survive, and thrive.

JACKIE COLEMAN is a former marriage counselor and most recently worked on education programs for the state of Georgia. JOHN COLEMAN is the author of the *HBR Guide to Crafting Your Purpose* (Harvard Business Review Press, 2022) and coauthor of *Passion and Purpose* (Harvard Business Review Press, 2012). Subscribe to his free newsletter, *On Purpose*; follow him on Twitter @johnwcoleman; or contact him at johnwilliamcoleman.com.

Notes

1. Tom Rath and Jim Harter, "Exercise, Sleep, and Physical Well-Being," Gallup, October 21, 2010, https://news.gallup .com/businessjournal/127211/exercise-sleep-physical -wellbeing.aspx.
2. "Reading 'Can Help Reduce Stress,'" *The Telegraph*, March 30, 2009, https://www.telegraph.co.uk/news/ health/news/5070874/Reading-can-help-reduce-stress .html.

Adapted from content posted on hbr.org, May 28, 2019
(product #H04YTE).

4

The Right Way to Form New Habits

An interview with James Clear by Alison Beard

Developing good habits starts with self-awareness and discipline. When you make the active choice to read 10 pages of a book, work out for 30 minutes, or meditate every day, it can only be sustained by being aware of how this habit will benefit you not only that day but in the long run as well.

People who recognize how habits play into living a happier lifestyle understand that small efforts can make a huge impact. James Clear is an entrepreneur who recognizes the importance of habits. He is the author of *Atomic Habits: An Easy and Proven Way to Build Good Habits and Break Bad Ones.* In this interview, *HBR IdeaCast* host Alison Beard sits down with Clear to talk about how to develop habits that will benefit you right now and in the future—and overcome any emotional hurdles along the way.

Alison Beard: *You've written that we limit ourselves by saying things like, "I'm not a morning person," "I'm bad at remembering names," "I'm always late," "I'm not good with technology," and "I'm horrible at math."*

I say all of those things about myself, even though I know that waking up earlier, remembering names, being on time, and getting better at math and technology as a business journalist would make me much better in my job. How do I change that mindset about myself?

James Clear: This is the reason why habits matter: They can shift your internal narrative. They can change your self-image. The first time you do something—or the 10th time, or maybe even the

100th time—you may not think that about yourself or have adopted that fully. But at some point, when you keep showing up, you cross this invisible threshold. You start to think, yeah, maybe I *am* a studious person, or maybe I *am* a clean and organized person.

Every action you take is like a vote for the type of person you want to become. The more that you show up and perform habits, the more you cast votes for being a certain type of person, the more you build up this body of evidence to say, "Hey, this is who I am."

This is what makes my approach a little bit different from what you often hear about behavior change, which is something like "fake it till you make it." "Fake it till you make it" is asking you to believe something positive about yourself without having evidence for it. We have a word for beliefs that don't have evidence: delusion.

At some point your brain doesn't like this mismatch between what you keep saying you are and what your behavior is. Behavior and beliefs are a two-way street. My argument is that you should let the behavior lead the way. Start with one push-up, with writing one sentence, with meditating for one minute—whatever it is—because, at least in that moment, you cannot deny that you were the type of person who didn't miss workouts, you were a writer, or you were a meditator.

In the long run that's the real objective. The goal is not to run a marathon; it's to become a runner. Once you start assigning those new identities to yourself, you're not even really pursuing behavior change anymore. You're just acting in alignment with the type of person you see yourself to be. In that way, true behavior change is really identity change.

How can we bring this into a work context?

Specifically with work, we can broadly lump habits into two categories. The first category is habits of energy—for example, building good sleep habits. That's sort of a meta-habit that if you get that dialed in, you're in a better position to perform almost every other habit. If you're not well rested, then you're hindering yourself in your performance each day. Pretty much any health habit falls in that bucket. Exercise, stress reduction, or nutrition habits—they are all in the "habits of energy" bucket.

The second category, unlike the first, is directly related to knowledge work. I call them habits of attention. For almost all of us, and certainly for people who are spending their time doing knowledge work or who are paid for the value of their creativity, the ideas you come up with are often a product of where you allocate your attention. This means that what you read and what you consume often is the precursor to the thoughts that you have, or to the creative or innovative ideas that you come up with.

By improving your consumption or attention habits, you can dramatically improve the output that you have at work as well. We all live in this world that has a fire hose of information. The ability to curate, edit, and refine, to filter your information feed—whether that be the people that you follow on social media, the articles that you browse each day, the news sources that you select, or the books that you read—is an important decision that determines downstream output.

Still, there are also other habits you can build, ones whose purpose is not to bring things in but to cut things out, like distractions. For example, one habit that I've been following for the last year or so is leaving my phone in another room until lunch each day. I have a home office and if I keep my phone on my desk, I will check it every three minutes just because it's there. But if I leave it in another room, I never go get it.

We see this so much with habits of technology and convenience in modern society, particularly with smartphones or apps. Actions are so simple that we find ourselves being pulled into them, at the slightest whim. Just the faintest hint of desire is enough to pull us off course. If you can redesign your environment, whether it's your desk at work or your home office, you can classify the actions of least resistance as the good and productive ones. You can increase the friction of the things that take your attention away.

You often find those habits of attention start to be allocated to more productive areas as well. But I would probably say habits of energy and attention are the two places to focus if you want to increase your work output.

OK, so you've taken that first step. How do you build from there to more significant, visible progress?

At some point you want to advance to where that progress is visible to everyone. This is what I call habit graduation. You want to step up to the next level. My general rule of thumb is to get 1% better each day. The way that money multiplies through compound interest is the same way the effects of your habits multiply when you repeat them over time. I like to say habits are the compound interest of self-improvement.

Take reading, for example. Reading one book will not make you a genius. But if you build a habit of reading every day, then not only do you finish one book after another, but with each book you complete, you now have a new frame or a new way to view all the previous books that you've read.

As you add more connection points and perspectives, knowledge starts to compound on top of itself. A lot of habits are like that—doing an extra 10 minutes of work each day, for instance. Maybe that's making one more sales call or sending one more email. Doing an extra 10 minutes on one day isn't really going to be very much. But the difference between someone who doesn't do that and someone who does an extra 10 minutes every day for a 30-year career can compound to a surprising degree. That one extra sales call a day can mean a lot over the course of years and decades.

If you have good habits, time becomes your ally. You just need to be patient. You need to let that compounding process work for you. But if you have bad habits, time becomes your enemy. Each day that clicks by, you dig the hole a little bit deeper and put yourself a little bit further behind the eight ball.

You argue vehemently that this is not a linear progression. There are going to be times when you stall or regress. How do you navigate that emotionally and keep pressing on?

The emotional part is a big factor my readers ask me about frequently. They'll say something like, "I've been running for a month, why can't I see a change in my body?" Or, "I've been working on this novel for five and a half months now and the outline's still a mess. Is this thing ever going to be finished?" When you're in the thick of the work, it's really easy to feel that way.

Sometimes I like to equate the process of building your habits to the process of heating up an ice cube. Let's say you walk into a room and it's cold—around 25 degrees. You can see your breath, and there's this ice cube sitting on the table in front of you. You start to slowly heat the room up to 26, 27, 28 degrees. The ice cube is still sitting there. It keeps going—29, 30, 31 degrees. Then you go from 31 to 32 degrees. This one-degree shift is no different than all the other one-degree shifts that came before it, but suddenly you hit this phase transition and the ice cube melts.

The process of building better habits and getting better results is often like that. You're showing up each day, and the degrees are increasing a little bit. You're making these small improvements. You're getting 1% better. But you don't have the outcome that you're trying for. Those delayed rewards haven't showed up yet.

So, although you feel like stopping, the process of giving up after doing a habit for a month or three months, or even six months, is kind of like complaining about heating an ice cube from 25 to 31 degrees and it not melting yet. The work is not being wasted; it's just being stored.

That's the kind of approach to take with your habits. It's not the last sentence that finishes the novel; it's all the ones that came before. It's not the last workout that gives you a fit body; it's all the ones that came before. And if you can be willing to keep showing up and keep hammering on the rock—to keep building up that potential energy, to know that it's not wasted, but that it's just being stored—then maybe you can start to fight that emotional battle of building better habits and ultimately get to the rewards that you're waiting to accumulate.

Why do good habits seem so hard to form and maintain, yet bad habits seem so easy to form and hard to break?

I thought about this a lot when I was working on *Atomic Habits*, because asking that question can reveal a lot about what we want to do to build a good habit or to break a bad one.

Let's say we want to build good habits. Well, why do bad habits stick so readily? What you find is they have a variety of qualities. First, they are obvious. For example, let's say that eating at fast-food restaurants is a bad habit or a habit that you don't want to perform as much. Well, in America it's hard to drive down the street for more than 15 minutes without passing at least a few, if not a dozen, fast-food restaurants. They're very prevalent in the environment. So that's a lesson that we can take and apply to our good habits. If you want a good habit to stick, then you should make it a big part of your environment.

Another quality bad habits often have is convenience. They're frictionless. The incredible convenience of many bad habits is a big reason why we stick to them so much. So if you want your good habits to stick, they need to be as easy and convenient as possible.

A third quality is that the rewards are usually immediate, while the cost they have is often delayed; with good habits it's often the reverse. For example, the benefit of going to the gym for a week is not a whole lot. You haven't really changed. You look the same in the mirror. The scale is roughly the same. It's only when you stick with it for a year or two that you get the outcome that you want.

There's sort of this valley of death in the beginning, where, when you start a lot of good habits, it's hard to accept that you won't be getting the rewards immediately. With bad habits it's the opposite. You get the immediate outcome. Bad habits feel great in the moment, but they ultimately hurt you in the long run.

The cost of your good habits is in the present. The cost of your bad habits is in the future. And a lot of the reason why bad habits form so readily and good habits form so slowly has to do with that gap in time and reward.

JAMES CLEAR is an author and entrepreneur. He is the author of *Atomic Habits: An Easy and Proven Way to Build Good Habits and Break Bad Ones.* ALISON BEARD is an executive editor at *Harvard Business Review* and previously worked as a reporter and editor at the *Financial Times.* Follow her on Twitter @alisonwbeard.

Adapted from "The Right Way to Form New Habits," *HBR IdeaCast* (podcast), December 31, 2019.

5

How Timeboxing Can Make You More Productive

By Marc Zao-Sanders

Years ago I read Daniel Markovitz's piece "To-Do Lists Don't Work" on migrating to-do lists into calendars. Since then, my productivity has at least doubled.

That momentous (at least for me) article describes five problems with the to-do list. First, they overwhelm us with too many choices. Second, we are naturally drawn to simpler tasks, which are more easily accomplished. Third, we are rarely drawn to important-but-not-urgent tasks, like setting aside time for learning. Fourth, to-do lists on their own lack the essential context of what time you have available. Fifth, they are missing a commitment device, to keep us honest.

This was enough for me. I converted from my religiously observed to-do list (daily work plan) to a calendar system, also known as timeboxing (a term borrowed from agile project management). All five of Markovitz's criticisms of to-do lists have become apparent to me. In a study we conducted of 100 productivity hacks, timeboxing was ranked as the most useful.[1] And over the last few years, I have also discovered several additional benefits of timeboxing that I would like to share.

First, timeboxing into a calendar enables the relative positioning of work. If you know that a promotional video has to go live on a Tuesday and that the production team needs 72 hours to work on your copy edits, then you know when to place the timebox. In fact, you know *where* to place the timebox: It's visual, intuitive, obvious. Working hard and trying your best is sometimes not actually what's required; the alternative—getting the right thing done at the right time—is a better outcome for all.

Second, the practice enables you to communicate and collaborate more effectively. If all of your critical work (and maybe just all of your work, period) is in your calendar, colleagues can *see* it. So not only are you more likely to plan your work to accommodate others' schedules (like in the previous example), others are able to check that your work schedule works for them. Shared calendars (with attendant privacy options) are the norm in the corporate world now, with Microsoft and Google leading the way.

Third, it gives you a comprehensive record of what you've done. Maybe you get to the end of a blistering week and you're not even sure what happened. It's in your calendar. Or a performance review looms— what were the highs and lows of the last six months? It's in your calendar. Or you're keen to use an hour to plan the following week and need to know what's on the horizon. It's in your calendar. Just make sure you have your own personal (i.e., not exclusively employer-owned) version of this data, or someday it won't be in your calendar.

Fourth, you will feel more in control. This is especially important because control (aka volition, autonomy, etc.) may be the biggest driver of happiness at work.[2] Constant interruptions make us less happy and less productive.[3] Timeboxing is the proper antidote to this. You decide what to do and when to do it, block out all distractions for that timeboxed period, and get it done. Repeat. Consistent control and demonstrable accomplishment is hugely satisfying, even addictive. This is not just about productivity (largely external); this is about intent (internal, visceral) and how we feel.

Fifth, you will be substantially more productive. Parkinson's law flippantly states that work expands to fill the time available for its completion. Although it's not really a law (it's more of a wry observation), most of us would concede that there is some truth to it (especially as it pertains to meetings). A corollary of this observation in practice is that we often spend more time on a task than we should, influenced by the time that happens to be available (circumstantial) rather than how long the work should really take (objective). Disciplined timeboxing breaks us free of Parkinson's law by imposing a sensible, finite time for a task and sticking to that. Although it's hard to precisely quantify the benefits of any time management or productivity measures, this is clearly enormous. Just take a commonplace example: Do you habitually take two hours (cumulatively, often drawn out over multiple sessions) to complete a task that really could have been done in a single, focused, timeboxed hour? If the answer is yes, then your personal productivity might be double what it is right now.

The benefits of calendarized timeboxing are many, varied, and highly impactful. The practice improves how we feel (control), how much we achieve as individuals (personal productivity), and how much we achieve in the teams we work in (enhanced collaboration). This may be the single most important skill or practice you can possibly develop as a modern professional, as it buys you so much time to accomplish anything else. It's also straightforwardly applied and costs nothing. Box some time to implement a version of this that works for you.

MARC ZAO-SANDERS is the CEO and cofounder of filtered .com, a company that blends consultancy with technology to lift capabilities and drive business change.

Notes

1. "The Definitive 100 Most Useful Productivity Tips," filtered, https://learn.filtered.com/hubfs/Definitive%20100%20Most%20Useful%20Productivity%20Hacks.pdf.
2. Belle Beth Cooper, "Autonomy Could Be the Key to Workplace Happiness," World Economic Forum, August 15, 2016, https://www.weforum.org/agenda/2016/08/autonomy-could-be-the-key-to-workplace-happiness.
3. "Are Digital Distractions Harming Labour Productivity?" *The Economist*, December 7, 2017, https://www.economist

.com/finance-and-economics/2017/12/07/are-digital
-distractions-harming-labour-productivity; and "2018
Workplace Distraction Report," Udemy, https://research
.udemy.com/wp-content/uploads/2018/03/FINAL-Udemy
_2018_Workplace_Distraction_Report.pdf.

Adapted from "How Timeboxing Works and Why It Will
Make You More Productive," on hbr.org, December 12, 2018
(product #H04P5Z).

6

Ten Minutes a Day Can Change the Way You React

By Rasmus Hougaard, Jacqueline Carter, and Gitte Dybkjaer

eaders across the globe feel that the unprecedented busyness of modern-day leadership makes them more reactive and less proactive. There is a solution to this hardwired, reactionary leadership approach: mindfulness.

Having trained thousands of leaders in this ancient practice, we've seen over and over again that a diligent approach to mindfulness can help people create a one-second mental space between an event or stimulus and their response to it. One second may not sound like a lot, but it can be the difference between making a rushed decision that leads to failure and reaching a thoughtful conclusion that leads to increased performance. It's the difference between acting out of anger and applying due patience. It's a one-second lead over your mind, your emotions, and your world.

Research has found that mindfulness training alters our brains and how we engage with ourselves, others, and our work.[1] When applied, mindfulness fundamentally alters the operating system of the mind. Through repeated mindfulness practice, brain activity is redirected from ancient, reactionary parts of the brain, including the limbic system, to the newest, rational part of the brain, the prefrontal cortex.

In this way mindfulness practice decreases activity in the parts of the brain responsible for fight-or-flight and knee-jerk reactions while increasing activity in the part of the brain responsible for what's termed our *executive functioning*. This part of the brain, and the executive functioning skills it supports, is the control center for our thoughts, words, and actions. It's the center of logical thought and impulse control.

Simply put, relying more on our executive functioning puts us firmly in the driver's seat of our minds—and, by extension, our lives.

One second can be the difference between achieving desired results or not. One second is all it takes to become less reactive and more in tune with the moment. In that one second lies the opportunity to improve the way you decide and direct, the way you engage and lead. That's an enormous advantage for leaders in fast-paced, high-pressure jobs.

Here are five easily implemented tips to help you become more mindful:

- *Practice 10 minutes of mindfulness training each day.* Most people find mornings the best time to practice mindfulness, but you can do it any time of day. You can use a 10-minute guided mindfulness training program, a short mindfulness training manual, or a downloadable mindfulness app. Try it for four weeks.

- *Avoid reading email first thing in the morning.* Our minds are generally most focused, creative, and expansive in the morning. This is the time to do focused, strategic work and have important conversations. If you read your email as you get up, your mind will get sidetracked and you'll begin the slide toward reactive leadership. Making email your first task of the day wastes the opportunity to use your mind at its highest potential. Try waiting at least 30 minutes, or even an hour, after you get to work before checking your inbox.

- *Turn off all notifications.* The notification alarms on your phone, tablet, and laptop are significant contributors to reactive leadership. They keep you mentally busy and put you under pressure, thereby triggering reactionary responses. They cause far more damage than they add value. Try this: For one week turn off email notifications on all of your devices. Only check your email once every hour (or as often as responsibly needed for your job), but don't compulsively check messages as they roll into your inbox.

- *Stop multitasking.* It keeps your mind full, busy, and under pressure. It makes you reactive. Try to maintain focus on a single task, and then notice when you find your mind drifting off to another task—a sign that your brain wishes to multitask. When this happens, mentally shut down all the superfluous tasks entering your thoughts while maintaining focus on the task at hand.

- *Put it on your calendar.* Schedule a check-in with yourself every two weeks to assess how well you're doing with the previous four tips or as a reminder to revisit this piece to refresh your memory. Consider engaging one of your peers to do the same thing. This gives you a chance to assess each other, which can be both helpful and motivating.

We encourage you to give these tips a try. Although mindfulness isn't a magic pill, it will help you more actively select your responses and make calculated choices instead of succumbing to reactionary decisions.

RASMUS HOUGAARD is the founder and CEO of Potential Project, a global leadership, organizational development, and research firm serving Microsoft, Accenture, Cisco, and hundreds of other organizations. JACQUELINE CARTER is a senior partner and the North American director of Potential Project. She works with senior leaders in global companies to enhance human potential and create more human workplaces. Hougaard and Carter are the coauthors of *Compassionate Leadership* and *The Mind of the Leader* (Harvard Business Review Press, 2021 and 2018, respectively). GITTE DYBKJAER is the director and partner of Potential Project Denmark. She is the coauthor of the Danish edition of *The Mind of the Leader*. Gitte has more than 20 years of solid experience facilitating leadership and organizational development.

Note

1. Tom Ireland, "What Does Mindfulness Meditation Do to Your Brain?" *Scientific American*, June 12, 2014, https://blogs.scientificamerican.com/guest-blog/what-does-mindfulness-meditation-do-to-your-brain/.

Adapted from "Spending 10 Minutes a Day on Mindfulness Subtly Changes the Way You React to Everything," on hbr.org, January 18, 2017 (product #H03EGU).

7

Prevent Burnout by Making Compassion a Habit

By Annie McKee and Kandi Wiens

"**I** am sick to death of the ridiculous situations I have to deal with at work. The pettiness, the politics, the stupidity—it's out of control. This kind of thing stresses me out to the max."

Stress is a happiness killer. And life is just too short to be unhappy at work. But we hear this kind of thing all the time from leaders in industries as varied as financial services, education, pharmaceuticals, and health care. In our coaching and consulting, we're seeing a spike in the number of leaders who used to love their jobs but now say things like, "I'm not sure it's worth it anymore." They're burned out—emotionally exhausted and cynical—as a result of chronic and acute work stress.

Why is stress on the rise? A lot of it has to do with uncertainty in the world and constant changes in our organizations. Many people are overworking, putting in more hours than ever before. The lines between work and home have blurred or disappeared. Add to that persistent (sometimes even toxic) conflicts with bosses and coworkers that put us on guard and make us irritable. Under these circumstances, our performance and well-being suffer. Work feels like a burden. Burnout is just around the corner. And happiness at work is not even a remote possibility.

Here's the good news: Some people *don't* get burned out. They continue to thrive despite the difficult conditions in their workplace.

Why? The answer lies in part with empathy, an emotional intelligence competency packed with potent stress-taming powers. Empathy is "compassion in action." When you engage empathy, you seek to understand people's needs, desires, and point of view. You feel and express genuine concern for their well-being, and then you act on it.

One of our studies (Kandi's research on executive-level health-care leaders) confirms this.[1] When asked how they deal with chronic and acute work stress, 91% of the study's executives described how expressing empathy allows them to stop focusing on themselves and connect with others on a much deeper level. Other researchers agree: Expressing empathy produces physiological effects that calm us in the moment and strengthen our long-term sustainability.[2] It evokes responses in our body that arouse the (good) parasympathetic nervous system, and it reverses the effects of the stress response brought on by the (bad) sympathetic nervous system. So not only do others benefit from our empathy, but we benefit, too.

Based on our research, Annie's with leaders in global companies and Kandi's with health-care leaders, we offer a two-part strategy that can help unleash empathy and break the burnout cycle. First, you need to practice self-compassion. Then you will be ready to change some of your habitual ways of dealing with people so you—and they—can benefit from your empathy.

Practice self-compassion

If you really want to deal with stress, you've got to stop trying to be a hero and start caring for and about yourself. Self-compassion involves: (1) seeking to truly understand yourself and what you are experiencing emotionally, physically, and intellectually at work; (2) caring for yourself, as opposed to shutting down; and (3) acting to help yourself. Here are two practical ways to practice self-compassion.

Curb the urge to overwork

When the pressure is on at work, we're often tempted to work more hours to "get on top of things." But overwork is a trap, not a solution. Just doing more—and more, and more, and more—rarely fixes problems, and it usually makes things worse, because we are essentially manufacturing our own stress. We shut the proverbial door on people and problems, thinking that if we can get away, we can at least do our job without getting caught up in others' drama. When nothing changes or it gets worse, we give up. This is a vicious cycle: Overwork leads to more stress, which leads to isolation, which causes us to give up, which leads to even more stress. So, instead of putting in more hours when you're stressed, find ways to renew yourself. Exercise, practice mindfulness, spend more time with loved ones, and—dare we say—get more sleep.

Stop beating yourself up

Stress is often the result of being too hard on ourselves when we fail or don't meet our own expectations. We forget to treat ourselves as living, breathing, feeling human beings. Instead of letting self-criticism stress you out, acknowledge how you feel, realize that others would feel similarly in the same situation, and be kind and forgiving to yourself. Shifting your mindset from *threatened* to *self-compassion* will strengthen your resiliency.

Give empathy

Taking steps toward self-compassion will prepare you emotionally to reach out to others. But let's face it: Empathy is not the norm in many workplaces. In fact, lack of empathy, even depersonalization of others, are symptoms of the emotional exhaustion that comes with burnout. Here are a few tips to make empathy part of your normal way of dealing with people at work.

Build friendships with people you like at work

Most people can rattle off a dozen reasons why you shouldn't be friends with people at work. We believe just the opposite. Real connections and friendships at work matter—a lot. According to the Harvard Grant Study, one of the longest-running longitudinal studies of human development, having warm relationships is essential to health, well-being, and happiness.[3] Other research shows that caring for and feeling cared for by others lowers our blood pressure, enhances our immunity, and leads to better overall health.

Value people for who they really are

The "ridiculous situations" mentioned by the leader at the beginning of this chapter are often the result of miscommunication and misunderstanding. Instead of really listening, we hear what we want to, which is misinformed by biases and stereotypes. It gets in the way of our ability to understand and connect with others. The resulting conflicts cause a lot of unnecessary stress. To prevent this, be curious about people. Ask yourself, "How can I understand where this person is coming from?" Listen with an open mind so that you gain their trust, which is good for your stress level and your ability to influence them.

Coach people

According to research by Richard Boyatzis, Melvin Smith, and 'Alim Beveridge, coaching others has positive psychophysiological effects that restore the body's natural healing and growth processes and improves stamina.[4] When we care enough to invest time in developing others, we become less preoccupied with ourselves, which balances the toxic effects of stress and burnout.

Put others at the center of your conversations

If misaligned goals with coworkers are a source of your stress, try physically moving your conversations to a place where you can put other people's needs at the center. One chief medical officer (CMO) who participated in Kandi's study described a time when he had an intense, stressful argument with two other physicians about the treatment plan for a terminally ill cancer patient. They were in a conference room debating and debating, with no progress on a decision. Seeing that everyone's professional conduct was declining and stress levels were rising, the CMO decided to take the conversation to the patient's room. He sat on one side of the patient's bed, holding her hand. The other two physicians sat on the opposite side of the bed, holding her other hand. They began talking again, but this time *literally* with the patient at the center of their conversation. As the CMO said, "The conversation took on a very different tone when we were able to refocus. Everyone was calm. It brought us to the same level. We were connected. It was a very effective antidote to stress."

One caution about empathy and compassion: They can be powerful forces in our fight against stress—until they aren't. Caring too much can hurt. Overextending your empathy can take a toll on your emotional resources and lead to compassion fatigue, a phenomenon that occurs when compassion becomes a burden and results in even more stress. So pay close attention to your limits and develop strategies to rein in excessive empathy if it gets out of control.

It's worth the risk, though. Once you commit to caring about yourself, you can start to care about others, and in the process you will create resonant relationships that are both good for you and good for the people you work with.

ANNIE MCKEE is an adjunct professor at the University of Pennsylvania Graduate School of Education and an adviser to global leaders. She is the author of *How to Be Happy at Work* and the coauthor of *Primal Leadership, Resonant Leadership,* and *Becoming a Resonant Leader.* KANDI WIENS is a senior fellow at the University of Pennsylvania Graduate School of Education, where she is the codirector of the Penn Master's in Medical Education Program and Penn Health Professions Education Certificate Program. She has extensive teaching experience in various Wharton Executive Education programs and in the PennCLO Executive Doctoral Program, and she is an executive coach and national speaker. Her forthcoming book, *Burnout Immunity*, will be published in 2024.

Notes

1. Kandi J. Wiens, "Leading Through Burnout: The Influence of Emotional Intelligence on the Ability of Executive Level Physician Leaders to Cope with Occupational Stress and Burnout" (PhD diss., University of Pennsylvania, 2016), https://www.proquest.com/docview/1848147162?pq -origsite=gscholar&fromopenview=true.
2. Kathryn Birnie, Michael Speca, and Linda E. Carlson, "Exploring Self-Compassion and Empathy in the Context of Mindfulness-Based Stress Reduction (MBSR)," *Stress & Health* 26, no. 5 (2010): 359–371; Helen Riess, "The Power of Empathy: Helen Riess at TEDxMiddlebury," TEDx Talks, YouTube video, December 12, 2013, https:// www.youtube.com/watch?v=baHrcC8B4WM; and Richard J. Davidson, "Toward a Biology of Positive Affect and Compassion," in *Visions of Compassion: Western Scientists and Tibetan Buddhists Examine Human Nature*, eds. Richard J. Davidson and Anne Harrington (Oxford: Oxford University Press, 2001).
3. Robert Waldinger, "What Makes a Good Life? Lessons from the Longest Study on Happiness," TEDxBeacon-Street, December 23, 2015, https://www.ted.com/talks/ robert_waldinger_what_makes_a_good_life_lessons _from_the_longest_study_on_happiness.

4. Richard E. Boyatzis, Melvin L. Smith, and 'Alim J. Beveridge, "Coaching with Compassion: Inspiring Health, Well-Being, and Development in Organizations," *Journal of Applied Behavioral Science* 49, no. 2 (2012): 153–178.

Adapted from content posted on hbr.org, May 11, 2017 (product #H03NLJ).

8

Building Healthy Habits When You're Truly Exhausted

By Elizabeth Grace Saunders

Forming a new habit in the best of times can be difficult, let alone trying to make changes when you're already spent. And you may find yourself exhausted and feeling doubtful that you can really turn your situation around—or simply confused about where to begin.

So what do you do when you're trapped in the vicious cycle of needing to improve your habits so you can feel refreshed but struggling to muster the willpower and motivation to even try?

In my experience as a time management coach, many of the individuals who come to me are already fatigued—sometimes to the point of burnout. They want change but don't know how to get started. So we need to find a path to recovery that honors their current state but doesn't leave them there.

The key to helping them move forward isn't coming down hard on them—they're already hard enough on themselves. Instead, what's most effective long term is to take a gentle, whole-person approach: Remembering the basics of taking care of yourself through sleep, nutrition, and exercise lays the foundation for you to then advance in other areas of time management.

If you find yourself utterly exhausted but longing for a change, here is the pathway to sustainably building new habits.

Start with sleep

If you're super tired, then the key to greater productivity is not to push harder, but to push less. Once you start getting enough sleep habitually, your body will support you in accomplishing your daily goals instead of dragging you down.

There's a very specific order in which I recommend working on sleep when you're at the point of exhaustion. Start with aiming for an earlier bedtime based on how many hours of sleep you need to be rested. If that's eight hours a night and you need to get up at 7 a.m., that means lights out at 11 p.m. Set a recurring alarm on your phone for around 30 or 45 minutes before that time to remind yourself to start winding down and prepping for shut-eye.

Once you begin to get the hang of heading to bed earlier, then start to work on your nighttime routine so that once you're lying down, you can actually fall asleep. Experiment with different strategies, such as signing off electronics an hour before bed, not watching anything too stimulating late at night, or simply dimming the lights.

The last step to improving your sleep quality is to focus on getting up at a consistent time. Most people put this goal as their first step, but it actually comes later in the process. I recommend this order because when you get to bed on time and fall asleep quickly, getting up is so much easier. And as an added bonus, consistently getting up earlier will help your morning routine run more smoothly on those days when you need to commute to the office.

Think about nutrition

Once you give yourself sufficient time to rest, then you'll start to have the capacity to work on other areas. I've found the next most effective habits for rebuilding energy involve simple nutrition strategies.

One effective habit is to start drinking more water. Greater water intake improves energy, aids concentration, and reduces fatigue and anxiety.[1] Make it a habit to always have a filled water glass or water bottle by you. I fill a water glass at breakfast, keep it on my desk while I work, and then keep refilling it throughout the day. If it's harder for you to do refills, get a really big water bottle so that you only have to fill your water container once for the day.

Then think about whether you're getting enough nourishment. Some of my coaching clients get so engrossed in their work or have so many back-to-back meetings that they don't feel like they have time to eat—or they simply forget to! If you find yourself in that situation, buy some simple nutrition options like bars or protein shakes that you always keep at your desk. Make it a goal to eat at least one or two during the day. As you're developing the habit, you may need to set a reminder on your calendar or phone, or place a healthy snack on your desk as a visual cue. My clients who have made remembering to eat a priority find that they have more energy throughout the day and end up feeling much less drained after work.

Get moving

With sleep and nutrition habits in place, start thinking about integrating in physical activity. Counterintuitively, exercise ultimately *gives* you more energy throughout the day instead of depleting it.[2] It also has the added benefits of improving mood, sleep quality, and focus.[3] Some of my coaching clients with ADHD find that exercise is one of the key ingredients to being able to concentrate throughout the day.

According to the Mayo Clinic, if you do at least 25 minutes of vigorous cardio exercise at least three times a week, you can improve your overall wellness. I recommend specifically dictating where and when you will do this exercise, such as, "I will work out Monday, Wednesday, and Friday from 7 to 7:30 a.m. at the gym." And if you find yourself struggling with motivation, find support through working out with friends, going to a class, or hiring a trainer. You can borrow the energy and motivation of others when you're feeling exhausted.

If that level of physical activity seems like too much to start, beginning with gentle stretching or walks is a step in the right direction. Make movement a ritual linked to a daily event such as, "When I get up, then I stretch for five minutes," to help you seamlessly integrate the habit into your lifestyle.

Pick a new habit

Attending to the basics of sleep, nutrition, and exercise will have improved your energy and focus during the day so that you have the capacity to take on more. Now you can pick other new habits to fold into your life.

To reduce the possibility of becoming overwhelmed, I advise choosing just one to focus on at a time. For example, you may decide to work on being on time, planning your week, breaking down projects, keeping up on email, or some other habit that you would like to master. Then emphasize incremental change. For instance, with being on time, you may pick one type of meeting where you aim to arrive a couple minutes early and then gradually expand the scope to other activities in your professional and personal life.

The key to habit change, especially when you're truly exhausted, is to take it slowly and steadily: moving forward but not putting too much pressure on yourself at any one time. You won't be able to change all of your habits in a day. But with time, you can develop new habits that will help you regain energy, stave off fatigue, and build momentum for ongoing growth and development.

ELIZABETH GRACE SAUNDERS is a time management coach and the founder of Real Life E Time Coaching & Speaking. She is the author of *How to Invest Your Time Like*

Money and *Divine Time Management*. Find out more at www
.RealLifeE.com.

Notes

1. Joe Leech, "7 Science-Based Health Benefits of Drinking Enough Water," Healthline, reviewed June 30, 2020,
   https://www.healthline.com/nutrition/7-health-benefits
   -of-water.
2. "Exercise: 7 Benefits of Regular Physical Activity," Mayo
   Clinic, October 8, 2021, https://www.mayoclinic.org/
   healthy-lifestyle/fitness/in-depth/exercise/art-20048389.
3. Kristen Nunez, "13 Benefits of Working Out in the Morning," Healthline, reviewed July 10, 2019, https://www
   .healthline.com/health/exercise-fitness/working-out-in
   -the-morning.

Adapted from content posted on hbr.org, April 1, 2022
(product #H06XNG).

9

Break Bad Habits with a Simple Checklist

By Sabina Nawaz

When we're starting out on a new goal, we're full of energy and enthusiasm. We eagerly make changes and take steps in our new direction in the first few weeks. But as time goes on, the newness wears off. Our energy drains, and we lose sight of our goal. Ultimately, we slide back into the status quo.

No matter how sophisticated your strategies to rid yourself of bad habits and create good ones, you're less likely to succeed if you don't track and review your progress frequently. Noting your improvements each day encourages you to keep going. And by identifying where you're falling short, you'll notice patterns and make adjustments so you won't feel stuck in habits that feel unnatural or aren't producing real change.

Consider the example of Yi-Min, chief of staff for a CEO at a technology firm. Yi-Min's colleagues thought he was a poor listener who micromanaged and didn't respect the time of those around him. His boss wanted him to work on being more considerate and empowering others. After receiving some particularly stinging feedback from a colleague that confirmed what his boss had shared, Yi-Min vowed to be a better leader. Together, we crafted a plan to help Yi-Min achieve his goals.

Yi-Min started by creating three goals, one for each area of negative feedback he'd received. He aimed to listen better, reduce micromanagement, and value others' time. While these objectives were ambitious and commendable, they weren't measurable. We needed to identify ways for him to improve that he could monitor and track. Here is what we came up with:

- *Listen better.* Attend one meeting a day without devices.

- *Micromanage less.* Use delegation techniques during one-on-one meetings with his staff to loosen his control and empower them to take on new responsibilities.

- *Value others' time.* Limit instant messages to two a day among all colleagues.

Note that for each goal, he chose only a small task. Taking on large tasks, or too many tasks at once, overwhelms us. You're more likely to follow through if the task is small. Once successful, you can then try a new activity or increase the original task's complexity. For example, in order to listen better, Yi-Min could have left all devices behind for *every* meeting, but that would be a hard shift to make. Instead, he started with one meeting a day. From there, he was able to decide whether to increase the number of device-free meetings or consider another activity that could help him to be a better listener.

Once he identified his tasks, it would have been easy for Yi-Min to move on with his daily work, with a plan to execute each of them. But this would have been a mistake. He would likely have started strong but slowly lost his dedication, distracted by daily to-dos and falling back into his old habits. Instead, Yi-Min needed to proactively track his daily progress.

I recommend using a simple tracking chart called the "Yes List" to help you see where you're making progress toward change and where you may be falling short. If you're groaning at the thought of a daily exercise, don't worry; this will take you no more than two minutes a day.

Simply track whether you accomplished each habit daily in a checklist, using Y for yes and N for no. For example, see Yi-Min's list in table 1.

TABLE 1

Yi-Min's "Yes List"

One executive tracks progress toward meeting three of his behavioral goals.

Goal	January													
	4	5	6	7	8	11	12	13	14	15	18	19
Attended one device-free meeting	Y	Y	Y	Y	Y	Y	Y	Y	Y	Y	Y	Y
Used delegation dial	N	N	Y	Y	Y	N	Y	Y	Y	Y	N	Y
Sent two or fewer IMs	Y	Y	Y	Y	Y	N	Y	Y	N	N	Y	N

Save your Yes List on your device or pin it as a hard copy somewhere you will see it regularly, and create a daily reminder to fill it out at the end of the day. Tracking your results allows you to see progress with a quick glance. Most people get a sense of accomplishment as they tally up the Y's and N's at the end of the day.

After several weeks of tracking your habits, assess whether there are any patterns that need adjusting. Doing so lets you see your successes—and missteps—and helps you to identify what might be causing issues.

For example, when Yi-Min and I reviewed his patterns, he found that he failed to delegate appropriately on Mondays. He realized it was because, at the beginning of each week, he met with the one employee who was an underperformer. Yi-Min was afraid to delegate to this employee because he feared receiving poor work in return. Once he understood this, he had a very different conversation during their next one-on-one. He gave more direct feedback instead of indirectly taking over the employee's work. Had he failed to notice the trend, he may never have addressed the real reason behind his challenges in delegating.

Reviewing his patterns also allowed Yi-Min to recognize when he was ready to introduce another habit aimed at achieving his goal. After practicing with one meeting a day, Yi-Min slowly increased the number of device-free meetings he attended until, four months later, he no longer used devices in meetings at all. He even stopped tracking his device-free meetings because it had successfully become a habit. He now had the energy and focus to tackle a new habit. Yi-Min replaced the old objective on the chart with the next one in his goal of being a better listener: paraphrasing what he heard at least once a day. He continued the pattern of creating a habit and adding a new one for each of his three goals. A year later, Yi-Min's staff consider him to be a stronger listener, a mindful collaborator, and an empowering manager.

You can set goals to achieve your dreams or improve your behavior, but without actionable ways to move forward and a method to measure progress, you'll fall back into your old bad habits once again. Take the time to identify how to meet your goals, starting with little steps, and take note of your improvements. Pretty soon, you may discover you've developed some positive new work habits.

SABINA NAWAZ is a global CEO coach, leadership keynote speaker, and writer working in over 26 countries. She advises C-level executives in *Fortune* 500 corporations, government agencies, nonprofits, and academic organizations. Sabina has spoken at hundreds of seminars, events, and conferences, including TEDx, and has written for the *Wall Street Journal, Fast Company, Inc., Forbes*, and *Harvard Business Review.* Follow her on Twitter @sabinanawaz.

Adapted from content posted on hbr.org, February 10, 2017 (product #H03FN8).

10

What Separates Goals We Achieve from Goals We Don't

By Kaitlin Woolley and Ayelet Fishbach

The importance of delaying gratification is universally recognized. Being able to forgo immediate benefits in order to achieve larger goals in the future is viewed as a key skill. For example, consider the classic marshmallow test experiment: Children's ability to delay eating one marshmallow so that they can get two marshmallows later is linked to a number of positive life outcomes, including academic success and healthy relationships.[1]

But wouldn't immediate benefits also help us follow through on our long-term goals? To explore this question, we conducted five studies, surveying 449 people, including students, gym-goers, and museum visitors. They reported their ability to persist in their long-term goals. They also told us whether they experienced immediate and delayed benefits when working toward these goals. (Our paper was published in the *Personality and Social Psychology Bulletin*.)

In one study, we asked people online about the goals they set at the beginning of the year. Most people set goals to achieve delayed, long-term benefits, such as career advancement, debt repayment, or improved health. We asked these individuals how enjoyable it was to pursue their goal, as well as how important their goal was. We also asked whether they were still working on their goals two months after setting them. We found that enjoyment predicted people's goal persistence two months after setting the goal far more than how important they rated their goal to be.

Yet people overestimated how much delayed benefits influenced their goal persistence. When we asked people what would help them stick with their goal in the upcoming months, they believed both immediate and delayed benefits—enjoyment and importance—

mattered for their success. In actuality, delayed benefits had less influence on persistence; they mainly played a role in setting the goal in the first place.

We found this pattern—immediate benefits are a stronger predictor of persistence than delayed benefits—across a range of goals in areas including fitness, nutrition, and education. In one study, we measured the number of minutes gym-goers spent exercising on a cardio machine. We also asked them how much they cared that their exercise improved their health (delayed benefit) and was fun (immediate benefit). Gym-goers who cared more about having a fun workout exercised longer than those who cared less about having fun. Caring more about the delayed health benefits of their exercise, such as staying fit, did not affect how many minutes they spent on a cardio machine.

A similar pattern appeared in another study we conducted measuring adherence to healthy habits over time. We approached Chicagoans who were visiting a museum and asked them to rate how much they enjoyed exercising, as well as how many hours per week they exercised over the last three months. Those who rated exercising as more fun exercised more each week over that period. The extent to which these people thought exercising was important for their health goals did not predict the amount of time they spent exercising over that period. Although people reported that exercising was both important and fun, importance did not predict their exercise behavior; having fun did.

We also asked these same museum visitors about their healthy food consumption. They rated the tastiness and importance of eating green vegetables and reported their weekly vegetable consumption. People who really liked the taste of vegetables also reported eating more servings over a one-week period. However, rating green vegetables as more important for their health did not lead to greater consumption.

This effect also appeared when we looked at University of Chicago students' persistence in studying. Most students study to receive delayed benefits, such as good grades. But studying can also provide enjoyment if the topic is interesting. We asked students working at the University of Chicago library how much they enjoyed their study materials and how important their study materials were for success in their classes. Whereas those who enjoyed their materials more spent more time studying, there was no relationship between the importance of the materials and time spent studying. Even though students study because it is important, this is not what predicted their study behavior.

Harness immediate benefits to increase your persistence

How can we use these findings to help people follow through with important goals? Other research we conducted, through four experiments and a sample of 800 students and adults, offers three strategies.

First, factor in enjoyment when choosing which activity to pursue to achieve your goals. For example, choosing a weight-lifting exercise based on enjoyment led gym-goers to complete more repetitions of their exercise. On average, they completed 52% more repetitions of the exercise they selected based on enjoyment versus one they selected based on effectiveness. So, if you want to work out more, select a fitness class that you enjoy. If you want to succeed at work, find a work task or a work environment that you enjoy. And if you want to eat healthier, build a diet plan around healthy foods you actually like to eat.

Second, give yourself more immediate benefits as you pursue long-term goals. We found that high school students worked longer on a math assignment when they listened to music, ate snacks, and used colored pens while working. Immediate benefits make difficult tasks seem less like work and more like fun.

Making activities more enjoyable, by listening to music while exercising or working in your favorite coffee shop, may help you persist in your goals.

Third, reflect on the immediate benefits you get while working toward your goal. For example, we found that people ate almost 50% more of a healthy food when they focused on the positive taste, compared with another group that focused on the health benefits. When you are pursuing a goal, seeking out the positive experience—to the extent that it offers one—may aid your persistence.

Setting a goal is the first step toward achieving the delayed outcomes you want. Yet, forgoing immediate outcomes or daily pleasures can undermine these goals. By making the experience more rewarding in the moment, you'll have a better chance at success.

KAITLIN WOOLLEY is an associate professor of marketing at the Johnson Graduate School of Management at Cornell University. AYELET FISHBACH is the Jeffrey Breakenridge Keller Professor of Behavioral Science and Marketing at the

University of Chicago's Booth School of Business and the author of *Get It Done: Surprising Lessons from the Science of Motivation.*

Note

1. Walter Mischel, Yuichi Shoda, and Monica L. Rodriguez, "Delay of Gratification in Children," *Science* 244, no. 4907 (1989): 933–938.

Adapted from content posted on hbr.org, April 26, 2017 (product #H03MLT).

11

Celebrate to Win

By Whitney Johnson

A s adults, we are often much better at work than we are at play. In fact, we seem to turn play into a form of work, one at which we are sadly less competent. Take, for example, office retirement and birthday parties, complete with balloons, pastries, and the requisite crudité platter. It's usually a drop-by-between-meetings party. Say hi. Grab a plate of goodies to eat, alone, at your desk. Even the guest of honor may only do a fly-by.

At Disruption Advisors we have found that most of us don't have a good plan to celebrate accomplishments, and the lack of celebration has only become more pronounced and consequential after pandemic isolation. This is unfortunate because, as I explain in my book, *Smart Growth*, celebration is an important opportunity to cement the lessons learned on the path to achievement and to strengthen the relationships between people that make future achievement more plausible. When I speak of celebration, I don't mean inebriated partying, but rather commemorative events that encompass complex emotions including solemnity and poignancy, as well as pleasure and joy in the journey.

Every initiative—or growth journey—we undertake, whether personal or professional, can be modeled by an S curve of learning. At the base of the S we are on a launch point where we encounter fruitful struggle. Resources and expertise may be in short supply. Growth is slow, sometimes hard to discern, but it is happening. Small, achievable goals and appropriate metrics help us see momentum and experience early victories. As expertise and momentum build, we tip into a sweet spot of competence, a phase of rapidly accelerating progress and productivity. Many projects may come to successful completion during this time. Eventually, however, our growth slows as we approach mastery. The top of the S can be a danger zone of boredom and stagnation. It's time for a new challenge.

Eventually we do have to move on to a new challenge, but it's important to remember that celebration is itself an important milestone on the S curve, whether it's an individual's, a team's, or an entire organization's S curve.

As I said, most organizations do not seem to have a celebration strategy, and individuals also have an "on to the next" mindset, as though it is contrary to productivity and efficiency to relish, even briefly, reaching our objectives. Nothing could be further from the truth.

Fortunately, it's easy to integrate celebration into your life and organization. Start with these four strategies.

Celebrate early and small

Progress is hard won early in a challenge (the launch point on the S curve). It can be discouraging and require painful perseverance. So why wouldn't we celebrate the early victories, no matter how small? Leading behavioral scientist BJ Fogg explains the link between emotions and habits. Habit formation is not, as conventional wisdom claims, a matter of 21 days of consistent practice. Celebrating small wins stimulates dopamine release in the brain, a feel-good chemical that reinforces the learning experience and strengthens our sense of connection to those we work with. Change and growth are promoted through positive emotions more than through disciplined practice. Keep in mind that celebration is an experience, and, in the workplace, it is most effective when shared with colleagues. It is not a certificate, a gift card, or an employee-of-the-month parking spot, although those rewards may serve a purpose too.

Just as the accomplishments we celebrate don't have to be large, our celebrations don't have to be grandiose; they just need to be meaningful. Cancer patients completing a course of chemotherapy are encouraged to ring a bell while being applauded by involved health-care givers. This psychologically powerful acknowledgment, though small, should never be skipped.

Celebrate in the interim

The sweet spot of the S curve is the phase of greatest productivity. As an individual or leader, there are good reasons to want to extend this stretch of the curve for as long as reasonably possible. This can require reconfigured teams, stretch projects, and imposed constraints to keep the challenge level high enough to prolong growth and engagement. These techniques ensure that many smaller mountains will be scaled en route to the ultimate summit. Celebrate all of them. We don't just celebrate our first birthday and our last; we celebrate every birthday in between. Whenever an objective is achieved, have a plan to commemorate it, even if the actual objective and commemoration are modest. Make sure individuals recognize their own achievements and know that their managers and teams recognize and appreciate them too. Celebration reinforces lessons learned and practices adopted, and strengthens the foundation and esprit de corps for future accomplishments.

Celebrate at the top

This seems obvious, but apparently it isn't. For an example, consider the typical retirement celebration described earlier. Even for the big, ultimate events, we struggle to hit pause on our busyness to truly acknowledge the mountain conquered. Fred B. Bryant describes celebrating his victory atop Snowmass

Mountain in Colorado in his book *Savoring: A New Model of Positive Experience*, coauthored with the late Joseph Veroff. Bryant had attempted the climb twice previously, without success. He knew it was unlikely he would ever return. So he lingered with his friends, taking in the spectacular view, and committing the sensations of the moment to memory: the smell of the air, the sound of the wind, the details of the scenery. He mentally reviewed the challenges he had overcome to reach this moment. Then he embraced his friends—his climbing colleagues—and expressed his gratitude to have shared the climb and the celebratory moment with them. In all, he spent about 10 minutes at the summit, basking in the joy and poignancy of the moment of mastery.

Your mountain might be landing a dream job, launching a product, closing the deal with a big client, going public, or one of many common—but uncommon for you—events. The celebration need not be long or elaborate, but it must be meaningful.

Celebrate the day

Each day is an S curve of its own. I encourage you to think of them this way. Take a few moments in the morning before engaging in tasks—even before reading email—to think through the day to come. What is the most important objective to achieve today? This is the mountaintop, the summit of the day's S curve. Whatever else the day requires, keep this critical objective the top priority. The morning contemplation is your base camp from which to attack the climb. At the end of the day, celebrate achievement, or your progress toward it. BJ Fogg says celebration can be as simple as looking in the mirror and claiming, "Victory."

Feyzi Fatehi, CEO of Corent Technology, a frequent self-disruptor, and a literal climber of mountains, made this analogy when I interviewed him for the *Disrupt Yourself* podcast: "I always told myself when you feel too comfortable, you have to move. . . . It's like in climbing; you can't just camp somewhere. You can rest. You can look around. You can take a deep breath, have a snack. But you've got to keep moving, otherwise you get complacent."

Celebration is an event, not a destination. It's the little pause where we survey the road we've traveled and the mountain we've climbed. We can have a snack with our colleagues or friends, rather than alone in our office. We rest, we catch our breath, we contemplate the next opportunity ahead, before descending to climb again. But the fact that the interval is brief doesn't make it unimportant, or harmless if neglected. Celebrating achievements great and small is high-octane fuel for further achievement. We don't just celebrate the win; we celebrate *to* win.

WHITNEY JOHNSON is the CEO of Disruption Advisors, a tech-enabled talent-development company, and the author of *Smart Growth: How to Grow Your People to Grow Your Company* (Harvard Business Review Press, 2022).

Adapted from content posted on hbr.org, January 26, 2022 (product #H06U4Q).

Index

How to be human at work.

HBR's Emotional Intelligence Series features smart, essential reading on the human side of professional life from the pages of *Harvard Business Review*. Each book in the series offers uplifting stories, practical advice, and research from leading experts on how to tend to our emotional well-being at work.

Harvard Business Review Emotional Intelligence Series

Available in paperback or ebook format. The specially priced six-volume set includes:

- Mindfulness
- Resilience
- Influence and Persuasion
- Authentic Leadership
- Happiness
- Empathy